COLLINS AURA GARDEN HANDBOOKS

ORCHIDS

MOLL

D1471872

COLLINS

Products mentioned in this book

ICI Antkiller Dust	contains	pirimiphos-methyl
ICI Mini Blue Slug Pellets	contains	metaldehyde
'Kerispray'	contains	pirimiphos-methyl
'Mouser'	contains	brodifacoum

Read the label before you buy: use pesticides safely

Editors Maggie Daykin, Joey Chapter
Designer Chris Walker
Production Controller Craig Chubb
Picture research Moira McIlroy

First published 1990 by
William Collins Sons & Co Ltd
London · Glasgow · Sydney
Auckland · Toronto · Johannesburg

© Marshall Cavendish Limited 1990

British Library Cataloguing in Publication Data

Pottinger, Mollie
    Orchids. — (Collins Aura garden handbooks).
    1. Orchids
    2. Title
A CIP catalogue record for this book is available from the British Library

ISBN 0-00-412528-2

Typeset by Litho Link Ltd., Welshpool, Powys, Wales
Printed and bound in Hong Kong by Dai Nippon Printing
Company

Front cover: Cymbidium hybrid 'Aviemore' by John Glover
Back cover: Epipectis gigantea by Paul Harcourt Davies

CONTENTS

INTRODUCTION

Orchids are accepted to be the world's most exotic and fascinating flowers, with their extraordinary variety of sizes, shapes, colours and markings. An aura of mystery has surrounded them since they were first brought to the British Isles in the early eighteenth century and they have been the subject of many myths and misconceptions.

Misinformation about the original habitat of certain species was sometimes deliberately fostered by collectors in order to confuse possible rivals and myths investing orchids with sinister and evil powers were eventually disproved. Misconceptions about their needs in cultivation have been superceded by proper understanding of their structure and now it is possible for anyone with some knowledge of greenhouse management and general gardening experience to grow and flower a collection of orchids successfully.

TOP A feast for the eyes of all orchid enthusiasts – a choice display growing under glass at the specialist Burnham Nurseries.

ABOVE The visually stunning Orchid Garden in Singapore. Many of the warmer-growing genera are raised in Singapore and Hawaii.

Early enthusiasts To start growing orchids was akin to entering a world of romance and intrigue. The travels of the early and intrepid orchid collectors were filled with adventures in wild uncharted places, daring encounters with primitive peoples, almost unbelievable hardships – and even death – endured in the search for novelties to fill the greenhouses of wealthy amateurs. Orchid mania increased with each new discovery and exorbitant prices were sometimes paid for particularly desirable specimens.

Those days are now long past and while some rare or exceptionally fine plants can still be expensive, it is possible to purchase many quite reasonably, even from garden centres or supermarkets, though considerably more variety of choice will be found in an orchid nursery.

Originating in the Far East between 100-120 million years ago, the *Orchidaceae* form the largest family of flowering plants, with between 20,000-30,000 species growing in wild places throughout the world. Their widely varying ecological niches embrace the temperate climates of Europe and North America; tropical rain forests wherein it is always warm and humid; cooler montane regions where clouds envelop the plants each morning and evening; and arid areas where rainfall is usually seasonal and frequently spasmodic.

The first orchids to arrive were a great rarity, cultivated in botanic gardens and by those who could afford to pay trained staff to take care of their greenhouses. It was thought that they should be grown in stove houses so the gardeners of those early days unwittingly caused the untimely death of many hundreds of plants. Even now there is a popular misconception that all orchids grow in a hot and humid atmosphere. While this is true of a number of species there are a great many which would languish and die if kept under such conditions.

Hybridization A natural trait of the human race seems to be the urge to attempt improvement on the works of nature, with varying degrees of success. Just over 130 years ago a Dr John Harris, at that time working at the Devon and Exeter Hospital, suggested to John Dominy, the head grower at the nursery of Messrs Veitch, that there might be a way to effect hybridization of orchids. Dominy's pursuance of this idea proved successful and the first man-made hybrid orchid produced flowers in 1856.

Once it was learned that the making of hybrids was possible there was no looking back and the result has been a flood of hybrids, all of which are duly registered in *Sanders' List of Orchid Hybrids*.

Man-made genera Not long after the first hybrids were made between species, it was found possible to create plants by taking the pollen from a species in one genus and placing it on the stigma of one in another genus. New and wonderful mixtures of colour, shape and habit appeared in these man-made genera, to fill orchid houses with plants which were often easier to grow and flower than their parents.

The naming of these new genera was usually solved by combining the names of the parent genera; for example, a species of *Laelia* crossed with a species of *Cattleya* became a *Laeliocattleya* and when a third genus, *Brassavola*, was added the new generic name expanded further, thus making it *Brassolaeliocattleya*.

An example of excellent cultivation: *Vanda rothschildiana* 'Carl Busby' (CCC/ RHS). Note the many flowers, leaves along the whole stem and healthy roots.

Beyond combining three generic names the whole system became too clumsy and a new one was evolved using the name of a person and adding the suffix *ara* as in *Vuylstekeara*, a genus named in honour of C. Vuylsteke, a Belgian who was one of the early orchid hybridizers.

Awards In 1889 the Orchid Committee of The Royal Horticultural Society was formed and to this day the Committee continues to award orchid flowers on the basis of their degree of excellence and Certificates of Cultural Commendation to growers of flowering orchid plants showing overall qualities of exceptional cultivation.

The year 1893 saw the publication of *The Orchid Review*, the first journal devoted entirely to all aspects of orchids, their habitat, discovery, description and cultivation requirements. This useful and informative publication still flourishes for the enjoyment and edification of orchid growers throughout the world.

STRUCTURE AND GROWTH

Anyone wishing to cultivate these wonderfully varied and exotic plants will find it interesting – and helpful – to have some knowledge of their structure and of the ways in which they are propagated. It should be said, however, that propagation of orchids is not an easy business for the amateur and most prefer to buy from specialist nurseries.

LEFT Orchids grow well with ferns, as here, where the orchids are growing epiphytically on a tree trunk.

RIGHT A mass of roots from plantlets (familiarly referred to as 'Keikis') formed on the flower stalk of a *Pleurothallis* species.

Orchids are monocotyledons (the group of plants that germinate with only one cotyledon, or seedleaf, like the grasses). The orchid family is divided into two main growth habits, monopodial and sympodial.

In monopodial orchids the main stem lengthens, sometimes branching, throughout the life of the plant. Adventitious roots grow from nodes along the stem and flowering occurs on stems issuing from the nodes or leaf axils.

Sympodial orchids flower mainly on inflorescences from new growths which are formed along a woody rhizome and rooting occurs from the base of these new growths. On many sympodial orchids the base of the stem is swollen to form a pseudobulb, a bulb-like structure which is in some species round or egg-shaped, in others shaped like an elongated cone, or laterally compressed with sharp edges.

In some genera the pseudobulb is quite tall, looking more like a much thickened stem, and this can be cylindrical or fusiform (spindle-shaped with the centre thicker than the top or the base). The pseudo-bulbs act as storage organs to help the survival of a plant when insufficient water is available.

Roots In tropical countries many orchids grow epiphytically on trees, giving an impression that they are parasites, like mistletoe. In fact, they merely perch upon the trees in order to get a better share of available light, well away from the usually crowded conditions on the ground. Epiphytic orchids often have lengthy root systems, in some cases travelling long distances along the branches or trunks of the trees they inhabit, clinging tenaciously and burrowing in rough bark so that it is often impossible to remove them without causing severe damage. Should the roots be badly damaged new ones usually grow, either from the plant or branching from above the broken part.

The roots are formed of a central core within an outer layer of spongy dead cells, called *velamen,* which can absorb moisture and nutrients very fast, storing them for quite some time. The velamen is often whitish or silvery but the growing root-tips are usually green or a rosy beige.

Leaves On some orchid genera, the leaves are flattish, ribbed lengthwise and thin-textured, often lasting only one season. Other genera have long-lasting leaves, hard and heavily fleshy, frequently V-shaped in cross section and sometimes quite thick and leathery. On the latter the stomata (microscopic pore-like openings which carry out gaseous interchange between plants and atmosphere) are mainly on the under surface so that water loss can be controlled, helping to prevent dehydration when moisture around the roots or in the atmosphere falls below the plant's requirement.

Leaves can be long or short, strap-shaped or elliptical, or even *terete* (round like a pencil). There are species in which leaves alternate up

ABOVE RIGHT Silvery roots on a monopodial epiphytic orchid. When the plants are resting, a sheath of dead cells (velamen) grows over the root-tips, indicating the need for reduced or even no watering.

RIGHT Orchid leaves with the bases covering the pendent stem.

LEFT Shown almost life-size, the leaves of *Phymatidium tillandsioides*, one of the miniature orchids. Despite their delicate form, the small white flowers are long-lasting.

BELOW Flower of *Cypripedium calceolus*, popularly known as the yellow Lady's Slipper or Moccasin Flower. Usually there are just two showy flowers per stem.

the whole stem and in some of these the leaf base clasps and entirely conceals the stem. Other orchids have leaves only at the top of their stem. The surface and edges of some leaves are smooth; on other plants they are downy or they may be edged with fine hairs.

Flowers The intricate form of orchid flowers is probably as much a part of their attraction as the long-lasting beauty for which they are famed. As with all monocotyledons, orchid flowers have their floral segments arranged in groups of three though this is not always readily discernable in all species. The three sepals are usually somewhat narrower than the inner ring of more colourful petals, two of which are fairly normal in shape while the third petal takes the form of a *labellum,* commonly referred to as a lip. The lip is, in most orchids, the most beautiful part of the flower; it is frequently spotted, blotched or striped with contrasting colour, in many genera bearing a raised crest near the base or having ornamental ridges along its length.

Some orchids have a spur, containing nectar, issuing from the base of the lip and usually pendent at the back of the flower; in others the petals are extremely small, the lip and column being well concealed within the more colourful sepals.

The shape of the flowers can be round and flat, the floral segments overlapping to a greater or lesser degree, or with segments narrowed and ribbon-like, often twisted, sometimes almost spidery in appearance; some flowers are tubular in shape.

There is almost endless variety of size and colour, though blue orchids are very rare – bluish-purple usually being a more accurate description – and on close inspection 'black' turns out to be the darkest shade of brown or purple.

Always, the flowers seem to have been designed with a particular pollinator in mind, for the shape and size of the lip is organized in such a fashion that it is just right for the pollinating agent, whether this is a bee, wasp, moth, or even, as in some cases, a bird or bat.

The reproductive organs are gathered into a column *(gynostemium)* in the centre of the flower. In most orchids the pollen is combined into small waxy masses, each on a thin stalk with a sticky pad at its base and hidden beneath a beaked cap at the tip of the column. The stigma takes the form of a cavity, filled with a sticky fluid, on the lower surface of the column.

Fertilization takes place when a pollinator, attracted by colour, shape or fragrance, lands on the lip and in crawling towards the centre of the flower dislodges the pollencap, allowing a pollen mass to adhere to its back or head ready for transfer to the stigma of the next flower it visits, thus ensuring that a flower is not fertilized with its own pollen. In common with most flowering plants the pollination mechanism of orchids favours crosspollination in order to preserve genetic strength, and there are certain species in which this takes quite elaborate forms.

The ovary is behind the other flower parts and after fertilization thousands of dust-fine seeds are formed. Some capsules ripen within a few weeks but others may take several months before they are ready to split lengthwise, releasing the minute seeds they contained, to be dispersed far and wide by even the lightest of breezes.

Seed The seed is lacking in nourishment to help the plant get started into growth, so thousands of seeds are formed in each capsule, relying upon a suitable substrate for their successful germination.

LEFT *Stanhopea eburnea* pushes its flowers through the slats in a hanging basket. If you grow it in a pot, you won't ever see the flowers, they will be buried in the compost.

RIGHT One of the very rare 'blue' orchids – and a particularly lovely one – *Vanda coerulea.* Vanda species may bear up to 12 or more flowers per spike on large plants.

LEFT Commercially grown orchids in sterile flasks. The advantage of buying them in this way is that they will be healthy; but they will need particular care when first removed from such an environment.

BELOW A selection of clones of the most successful hybrid *Pleiones*. These small plants are easy to grow.

PROPAGATION

In nature only a tiny amount of the seeds survive and this was also the case in the early days of orchid cultivation when seed was sprinkled on the compost surrounding the parent plant.

In vitro Modern methods of propagation in flasks ensure that the dust-like seeds stand a greater chance of survival and eventual germination. When using these *in vitro* methods of propagation it is vital to maintain a sterile atmosphere throughout the whole operation of seed-sowing, including thorough sterilization of flasks, the medium on which the seed is sown and even the seed itself, so the technique is usually left to those who have the facilities to surmount the sort of problems that this process entails.

Vegetative propagation It is not possible to increase a stock of orchids by taking 'cuttings' in quite the same way as with other plants. The usual method of multiplying a particular species or hybrid is by division, with sympodial orchids cutting the rhizome between growths or in the case of monopodial orchids removing a portion of the top after making certain that there are good, healthy roots already emerging from the section that is to be removed.

Meristem propagation When an orchid is thought to be particularly desirable it can be multiplied by the process of propagating from a meristem (the very tip of a growing point or growth bud). This involves stripping the growing point down to microscopic proportions in a clean air cabinet under sterile conditions and then culturing it in flasks, an expensive and time-consuming operation only used when the resulting plants will be a commercial success.

Conservation There is a growing awareness nowadays for the need to conserve wild plants (and animals) throughout the world, and orchids *are* at risk. The natural habitats from which they originate are now vanishing fast with the destruction of forests to make way for human needs. It is therefore imperative that as many species as possible should be nursery raised to reduce the pressure on wild populations.

This is a matter of concern for professional and amateur growers alike, and while progress is being made in this direction there is still a long way to go. Amateurs who do not feel able to propagate orchids themselves should therefore obtain nursery-raised plants whenever possible. It is, of course, an offence to remove or import protected plants such as orchids without the proper authorization and documentation.

LEFT Propagation by division is a technique applied to sympodial orchids with pseudobulbs. It is carried out in spring, when vigorous growth is beginning again and cuts will heal quickly. The plant should have made sufficient forward growth to reach the edge of the pot and overlap, as is shown here.

BELOW Remove any dead roots, then cut through the rhizome connecting the pseudobulbs, using a sharp knife. Plant up the divisions so that both have plenty of room for forward growth. This will come from a live eye on the back section, and from the already distinct new growth on the front section.

WHERE TO GROW

While a greenhouse is the usual place in which to grow orchids, allowing comparative ease in the matter of providing the correct conditions of warmth and atmospheric humidity, many fine plants are grown to perfection in garden-rooms or under artificial lights in basements or garages. Many people who live in centrally-heated flats grow orchids with conspicuous success on their windowsills and most orchid nurseries are usually happy to give you expert advice on which plants to buy for each circumstance.

Temperatures We have already noted that orchids originate in many parts of the world, from extremely hot and humid places in which low temperatures are never met with to regions where at times it can be uncomfortably cool, though actual frost would be of brief duration.

In high mountains the plants are drenched with moisture each morning as the sun draws clouds up from the valleys, then dry out during the day only to get another drenching in the evening when the clouds drop down into the valleys again. It is easily understood therefore that to cultivate the whole range of tropical orchids it would be necessary to maintain three main environments and a fourth if we consider growing the terrestrial orchids of Europe or other temperate climates.

Since most amateur gardeners seldom have more than one greenhouse or other suitable growing area the first priority is to consider what sort of conditions we are able to provide.

LEFT Orchids in flower can be displayed in an indoor cabinet, if a minimum temperature of 14°C (58°F) is maintained. Return them to their correct growing conditions when the flowers die.

RIGHT *Calanthe* 'Diane Broughton' was a favourite orchid of Victorian days, often grown in quantity and now making a come-back. It makes a long-lasting cut flower for indoor arrangements.

BELOW LEFT Correct temperature is crucial when growing orchids, so a maximum/minimum thermometer is an invaluable guide.

Heating When deciding which orchids to grow we need to decide how much heat we are willing to provide for their well-being. All plants grow best in the correct environment and while they will sometimes flower in a desperate attempt to reproduce themselves before dying, optimum flowering can be expected year after year only from healthy orchids.

The warmest growing section of orchids needs a minimum night temperature of 15-18°C (60-65°F). The next group is 'intermediate' and the requirement is for a minimum night temperature of 12-14°C (55-58°F). Then there are the 'cool' growing orchids needing 10°C (50°F) minimum night temperature, though some of the latter will tolerate a few degrees less provided that this is only for a short period of time.

All the temperature ranges should ideally experience a day lift of at least 5°C (10°F) and although all these figures are of necessity somewhat abitrary, a maximum/minimum thermometer is an invaluable guide to actual temperatures being achieved. The experience of many orchid growers favours the use of an electric fan-heater with internal or external thermostat, but gas- or oil-burning equipment can be perfectly satisfactory provided that it is properly installed and controlled.

It is essential to remember that electricity and water can be a fatal combination and all electrical installations should be undertaken by a qualified person.

LEFT A small orchid collection is here positioned on a gravel tray to retain moisture.

ABOVE Automated vents make it easier to keep the modern greenhouse efficiently ventilated.

Air movement It is desirable that the temperature should not exceed a daytime maximum of 32°C (90°F) for even the warmest-growing species and though this may be almost impossible to achieve on sunny summer days, overheating can be alleviated to some extent by use of a fan. It is noticeable that there is always some movement of leaves and flowers in the open garden even on a seemingly windless day and a similar situation can be simulated within the greenhouse by an oscillating fan which covers a wide area without blowing directly across the same plants all the time. This solution is preferable to opening windows or vents which would allow precious humidity to escape.

Even so, a greenhouse owner who cannot be at hand during the day may wish to install an automatic device set to open a roof vent at a pre-set temperature so that the plants do not suffer from undue heat-stress during such absence.

Humidity Orchids originating from such a vast range of environments often have different requirements with regard to humidity but it is safe to say that they all benefit from a degree of moisture in the atmosphere. Humidity can be created by thorough damping down of the greenhouse floor and staging early in the day, well before temperatures start to rise, and this should be done again later on hot days.

In winter some forms of heating tend to dry the atmosphere so, when it is cold and damp out of doors, the provision of humidity within the greenhouse would still be required. It is possible to ease the situation by installing a humidifier or a misting system beneath the staging, controlled by a timer or humidistat.

Insulation Awareness of the danger to our environment caused by burning fossil fuels, and the regular increases in the cost of electricity, gas and oil have contributed towards efforts to conserve energy by insulating our homes. This principle can also be applied to the greenhouse for very little outlay.

Although there is now a trend towards manufacturing double-glazed greenhouses, these are comparatively rare and of necessity rather costly. The most common form of insulation employed these days is the use of polythene sheeting fastened to the inside of the glass; ordinary sheet polythene is quite effective and easy to fix in position though many greenhouse owners have experienced better insulation by using bubble polythene. Fixing heavy-grade polythene entirely over the outside of the greenhouse is another effective method of reducing heat loss.

It must be remembered that in conditions of high humidity condensation could be a problem and drips falling on to plants could cause damage. Also, when contemplating any form of insulation, bear in mind that gas or oil heaters both require adequate ventilation.

Shading When spring brings us warmer days and the sun begins to rise higher in the sky it is quite possible that severe scorching of leaves and flowers may occur under glass. Shade paint or shade cloth should be applied at the beginning of spring (earlier if the situation demands) and the degree of shading should be dictated by the needs of the particular plants being grown.

In most cases it is possible to start removing shading by early autumn but again the timing should be determined by weather conditions. At the turn of the century, in the days of the great orchid collections, the head gardener would employ lads to open and shut vents, roll shading on or off and damp down as needed; nowadays we can use reliable automated mechanical help.

A collection of compatible orchids, grouped on wooden slats to aid good drainage and ventilation. Modern metal mesh from builders' merchants can be even more efficient, as it does not encourage slugs and woodlice.

CULTIVATION

Having taken care to create the correct conditions in which the orchids of our choice will flourish we can now get down to the more exciting and rewarding work of actually growing them. Choice of the right container and compost can make all the difference between a plant with live healthy roots and one which may hang on for months but eventually give up the struggle for survival and dwindle and die.

Cephalanthera-longifolia, a pleasing native form of the terrestrial orchids which can be seen growing wild. Do remember, if you have the luck to see such lovely plants, that all orchids are protected and should neither be picked nor completely removed. Leave them to be admired by others.

Roots are the life-lines of a plant, for in addition to their function of absorbing food and moisture they are the means by which it secures itself in the ground or, as in the case of epiphytic orchids, on the twigs or branches of a tree.

Though a few epiphytic orchids never seem to adapt to pot culture, the majority are much more amenable. The moisture-retaining quality of plastic pots is suitable for most situations, reducing the need for frequent attention to watering. Orchids originating from very arid places may prefer the faster drying property of clay pots, or a raft or basket made from wooden slats. Epiphytes which cannot adapt to pots or baskets may be fastened to pieces of cork bark or to fern fibre.

Compost The principal requirement of any orchid compost is for a certain amount of moisture retention allied to free passage of water through the container. A compost which has proved satisfactory over a number of years is composed of a mixture of conifer bark, such as ICI Forest Bark Chipped Bark, or coarse peat and charcoal with the addition of Perlite or Perlag. The proportions may vary according to each grower, some adding traces of organic fertilizers such as bone meal or hoof and horn. Ready-mixed composts can be purchased, if you prefer.

The use of rock-wool as a potting medium for orchids is comparatively new in this country though it has been used extensively on the European continent for some time. Mixed

18

with Perlite and sometimes a small amount of charcoal, it has no nutrient value so fertilizer must be applied frequently. It is also important to make certain that the fertilizer used contains the correct balance of nitrogen, phosphates, potassium and trace elements.

The terrestrial orchids from Europe, North America and Australia require a different compost from the epiphytes. A good basic mixture consisting of equal parts of unsterilized loam, fine bark and leafmould, to which are added 5 parts of horticultural grit, is suitable for the Australian species. A little more leafmould should be added when you are potting the others.

It is known that orchids have a symbiotic relationship with a mycorrhizal fungus and while this need not concern us most of the time, it is essential when repotting the cool-growing terrestrials to include up to half of the old compost along with the new mixture.

Watering This is often considered the trickiest part of growing orchids. A plant with storage organs like pseudobulbs needs to be watered thoroughly, then allowed to become dry before the next lot of water is applied. Orchids without pseudobulbs have to rely on moisture held in their stems and leaves, so watering should be more frequent.

There are orchids which will not flower unless they experience a definite, in some cases stringent, resting period when no water should be given. A useful guide to this frequently comes from the plant itself, for when it starts into active growth the root-tips show colour whereas velamen covers over the tips when growth is slowed down or the plant needs to rest.

Feeding Any balanced commercial fertilizer such as 'Kerigrow' used at about half-strength is adequate for feeding orchids but, bearing in mind that in nature the plants often have to rely on whatever minute amounts of nutrients may be dissolved in the rain trickling down a tree trunk, fertilizer prepared specifically for them and used in the concentration recommended on the label is always more satisfactory. The frequency depends on whether plants are in active growth or at rest. As with growing any pot plant, too much too often can be as bad as the opposite.

A nice wide range of epiphytic orchids, well established on cork bark, and displayed on trellis.

REPOTTING ORCHIDS

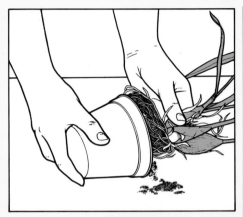

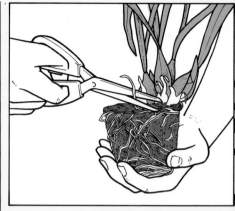

TOP LEFT When new growth overlaps the side of the pot, remove the orchid.

TOP Trim away any debris, taking care not to damage the plant.

CENTRE LEFT shows the need for repotting.

ABOVE Choose a new pot that is large enough to allow for further growth. Remove any old compost that shows signs of breakdown and position plant to one side of pot. Pour in fresh compost.

LEFT Give the base of pot a couple of sharp taps to settle the compost. Firm in.

Repotting When orchids are grown in bark-based compost it is best to repot annually just before new roots are about to enter the compost. This gives an opportunity to check on the state of old roots and make a note of whether any old leafless pseudobulbs should be removed. It is very rewarding when, after shaking off the old compost, a mass of healthy roots are revealed.

Alternatively, should overwatering or over-feeding have taken place for any length of time during the past year, the compost may have broken down to the extent that water cannot pass freely through the pot, thus causing roots to rot. When this happens any rotted roots should be stripped of velamen or cut off completely so that the rot will not be carried into new compost. Even in cases where nearly all the roots have rotted there is no need for despair; the orchids are more forgiving than most plants and new roots will almost certainly appear from the base of the next new growth.

The new pot should be just large enough to allow space for a year's growth and then it is a simple procedure to pour the bark mix around the roots and almost up to the pot rim. Some growers advocate thorough moistening of bark before using it, then not watering for a few days after potting; others use dry compost and apply water every day for a short while. Both methods work equally well.

Plants mounted on cork bark or fern-fibre blocks should be left undisturbed until they outgrow the piece of bark or fibre. It is a simple matter to tidy up the plant by cutting off any dead roots if they become unsightly.

Staking This should be carried out at an early stage, before the angle of the flowers is set. When staking, it is important to bear in mind the habit of the orchid – some spikes are pendent, some arching and others upright. Follow the plant's natural trend. Also, do not move the plant in relation to the light in which it has been growing or the flowers may open out in all directions instead of facing in the same way; the latter makes for a better display.

Insert the stake carefully so as not to damage the roots or the budding flower spike.

BELOW Having inserted the stake, make the first tie above or near to the pseudobulb. Add further ties as needed for support.

FAR BELOW Cut the stake down to size.

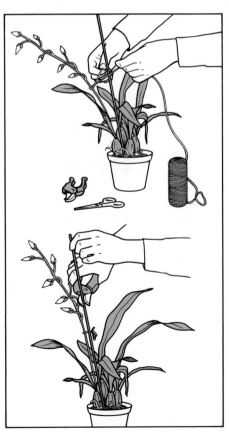

PESTS AND DISEASES

There are a few serious pests and diseases of orchids which can require treatment if they get out of hand. Be vigilant therefore, and pick off sick looking leaves and any insect pests large enough to see before the problem can spread. When a pest or disease is difficult to remove by this method, use an appropriate insecticide or fungicide spray to clear up the infestation. Apply a light, even cover and repeat the treatment as recommended until the problem is completely cleared. As a general rule, avoid treating open blooms.

PESTS

Aphids, scale insects and mealy bugs All of this group are sap-feeding pests which can weaken plants rapidly. Ideally pick them off by hand before they have a chance to increase in number.

If large numbers do build up then apply a light spray of 'Kerispray' to the whole plant (protecting any flowers as you do so).

Bush snails If new growths or flower buds appear to be damaged, look out for the very small bush snails (sometimes known as garlic snails because of the unpleasant odour they give off when they are crushed), which hide in the compost, coming out at night to satisfy their appetites. These shiny little pests can be removed when seen in the light of a torch.

Mice can be an unexpected hazard when Paphiopedilums (the slipper orchids favoured by many orchid growers) are about to flower, for they seem to find the pollens a gastronomic treat, biting into the buds to get at them. The best way to see mice off is to place a trap or a bait box such as the 'Mouser' close to

Although few pests and diseases attack orchids, it is important to pay attention to hygienic growing conditions for these exotic plants, at all times. If you are scrupulous in this respect, you should experience few – if any – of the problems outlined here.

Slug damage to flower buds

Mealy bugs and brown scale on leaves

the plant until the little beasts are despatched. Keep the trap or box in place until there is no sign of mice activity. Always handle traps with great care.

Snails or slugs Liquid slug killer or a few ICI Mini Blue Slug Pellets placed around each plant will be sufficient to deal with these, should they occur.

Vine weevils can be more troublesome, for they come out after dark to eat the flowers and when an attempt is made to remove them they drop down to become instantly lost in the compost. ICI Antkiller Dust or any diazinon-containing dust can be used around orchid plants and in the compost to prevent invasion by this pest. When using any insecticide always read the product label beforehand and follow the instructions carefully.

Woodlice The treatment suggested for vine weevils also applies to these little pests which seem to invade any greenhouse to worry the roots of plants, mostly during the night.

DISEASES

Fortunately, only a few diseases of orchids require special treatment.

Bacterial rot This slimy rot may appear around the base of the stem and bulbous growth. Carefully cut out infected material to healthy growth and then treat the wound with a copper-based fungicide dust.

Fungal diseases These can cause dark or light brown decay of the leaves, appearing in patches, often starting at the tips. Remove affected leaves or, if severe, treat with a copper-based fungicide.

Leaf spots There can be a wide range of causes, including environmental changes and fungi. No fungicide treatments are recommended for this problem. However, avoid excessive dampness, water on the leaves, draughts and direct sunlight.

23

SIXTY OF THE BEST

The following lists of orchids are arranged alphabetically in sections according to their temperature requirements, to make choice easy for those who are setting up an area where these fascinating plants will be grown. Some can be purchased at garden centres, supermarkets or large stores, but the widest variety will be found in specialist nurseries.

Ada aurantiaca has fiery orange flowers but likes cool conditions

The greatest pleasure and satisfaction will be had by starting a collection with plants in flower, or those which can be expected to flower soon, gradually adding younger plants or seedlings as more experience is gained. Among amateur orchid growers inflorescences are generally spoken of as 'spikes', so that is how they will be referred to in the following notes.

ORCHIDS FOR COOL CONDITIONS

Min. night temperature: 10°C (50°F)

Ada aurantiaca
This species, which comes from mountainous regions of Central America, has been in cultivation since it first arrived in Europe, in 1853, and bears its showy orange flowers in winter.

Coelogyne cristata
Discovered more than 160 years ago, this is the best known member of a genus comprised of over 100 species distributed through India and the Far East. The pendent spikes bear from 3 to 10 large snow-white flowers with a crest of golden-yellow ridges running down the centre of each lip. When well grown for a few years a large specimen will provide a spectacular display. Other 'cool' Coelogynes well worth growing include *C. massangeana* which has spikes of up to 30 creamy flowers with brown ridges on each lip.

Cymbidium hybrids
This genus with 44 species throughout India, China, Japan, Malaysia and parts of Australia is known for the superb hybrids seen at orchid shows in autumn and spring. Tall spikes rise from among the foliage to flaunt large flowers in shades of pink, yellow, green or white, the lips often beautifully marked. A new race of 'miniature' Cymbidiums has been bred and these are easier to accommodate in a small greenhouse.

26

Cymbidium devonianum

This, the most commonly grown species in the genus, was named in honour of the Duke of Devonshire, whose collector found it in the Khasia Hills in India, in 1837. The pendent flower spikes, up to 45cm (18in) long, carry many quiet coloured flowers, each of which measures about 3.5cm (1½in) across.

Cymbidium devonianum

Coelogyne cristata

Dendrobium nobile

Coming from N. E. India and S. China where it grows in full sun at altitudes up to 1500m, this is the most widely grown member of a genus comprising about 900 species from the Far East. Tall, thickened stems carry pale flowers 5-8cm (2-3in) across with pink-tipped petals, the lip nicely ornamented with a large dark area at its base. Considerable hybridizing, notably by Yamamoto in Hawaii, has produced flowers in a wide range of colours. The main requisite for good culture is plenty of moisture, light and warmth in the growing season and a severely cool rest from late autumn until flower buds begin to appear again in the early spring.

Dendrobium kingianum

This popular Australian dendrobium has small flowers varying from pure white to shades of pale or dark mauve-pink. A severe winter rest and maximum light, short of scorching, are needed to produce flowers instead of the small plantlets which are often produced at the top of erect, cylindrical stems.

Dendrobium nobile

27

Epidendrum ibaguense, a large plant without pseudobulbs

Dracula chimaera

Those who like unusual plants will enjoy this orchid. The plant must be grown in a hanging net-pot or slatted basket because of its habit of pushing flower stems downwards through the compost. The flowers are formed of the sepals, with each corner drawn out in a long tail; the tiny petals and shell-like lip sit neatly in the centre. The absence of pseudobulbs dictates that these cloud forest orchids should never be allowed to lack moisture around the roots or in the atmosphere.

Dryadella zebrina

This tiny plant with quiet coloured flowers nestling among the leaves is related to the Draculas but should be grown in a pot in the normal way; A cloud forest dweller, it needs moist roots and a cool humid atmosphere.

Encyclia citrina

Both leaves and flower spikes on this orchid are pendent. Complementing the daffodil-yellow flowers, its pale green leaves and stems are overlaid with a greyish bloom which rubs off if handled carelessly. It can be grown in pots or shallow pans but looks best mounted on bark. Plenty of water is needed when in growth.

Encyclia vitellina

With up to 20 vermilion flowers on upright spikes above blue-green foliage, this is a spectacular orchid from high elevations in Mexico and Guatemala. It should be grown in the coolest part of the greenhouse and the greatest care should be taken when watering not to allow spots to disfigure the attractive greyish bloom on the stems, leaves and pseudobulbs.

Epidendrum ibaguense

This orchid, which grows terrestrially throughout tropical America, has small, bright red flowers crowded on spikes at the top of leafy stems which eventually grow to well over 1m (3¼ft) tall. When conditions are favourable it seems to be always in flower.

Gomesa crispa

In spring and early summer this orchid will fill any greenhouse with the strong fragrance from dozens of yellowy-green flowers, each 1.25cm (½in) across, crowded on arching spikes up to 23cm (9in) long. It is important to pay attention to the free-draining property of the compost and, while needing shade from the hottest sun, it should be grown in the warmest part of the cool house.

Laelia anceps

The lovely flowers in this genus named after Laelia, one of the vestal virgins, are reason enough for its popularity for over 150 years. Large flowers of pale or rose-pink, at the top of 60cm (2ft) stems, create a picture of elegant simplicity. This spring-flowering orchid deserves a place in every cool greenhouse.

Masdevallia coccinea

This is the showiest and best known species in a genus named in honour of an 18th-century Spanish physician and botanist, Dr Jose Masdevall. The flowers consist of colourful sepals within which the small petals, lip and column are concealed. It has scarlet, magenta, white or yellow flowers singly at the top of 40cm (16in) stems, from among leaves 30cm (1ft) tall. The absence of pseudobulbs indicates that high humidity, a cool atmosphere and constant moisture around the roots are necessary for good cultivation.

Gomesa crispa 'Simla Jade'

Laelia anceps flowers in spring

Masdevallia coccinea

Odontoglossum 'Portlet Bay Trinity', each lovely flower palely outlined

Odontoglossum hybrids

The most famous of all Odontoglossum species is *O. crispum* with white, sometimes spotted flowers. First collected in the Colombian Andes in 1841, it did not become known until a further collection in 1863 when plants went to the Horticultural Society of London, Messrs Low of England and Jean Linden of Belgium.

John Day of Tottenham was the first person to grow and flower it successfully in cultivation and since then the species has continued to attract admirers both for itself and the hundreds of hybrids in which it is the major influence. With careful selection of parents in hybridizing, plant vigour and flower size has improved almost beyond recognition and the beautiful hybrids of today deserve pride of place in any cool house collection. Odontoglossums have also been bred with species from other related genera to make exciting bi-generic and multi-generic hybrids.

Odontoglossum rossii

This small species has lately been transferred to the genus *Lemboglossum*, but most orchid nurseries and amateur growers still refer to it as *Odontoglossum*. The showy white or pale pink flowers are large for a small plant; the base of the petals and the whole of the sepals are decorated with dark red spotting.

Oncidium ornithorhynchum

There are over 700 oncidiums in tropical and sub-tropical America and the plants range from a few cm (in) tall to very large specimens which require plenty of headroom

30

Oncidium ornithorhynchum

when in flower. All have a complicated crest on the lip and the golden yellow of the flowers, seen on many species in cultivation, is in others replaced by mauve, pinkish-mauve, white or rich brown. *O. ornithorhynchum* gives double pleasure in late autumn when the greenhouse is filled with sweet fragrance from clouds of small pink or mauve flowers on branched arching spikes.

Paphiopedilum insigne
The generic name of this group of about 60, mainly terrestrial orchids is derived from the Greek *Paphos*: an island on which there is a temple to Aphrodite, and *pedilon*: meaning slipper, roughly translating to 'slipper of Aphrodite' who was known to the Romans as Venus, the goddess of love and beauty. Thus the name 'Venus's slipper', or 'slipper orchid'

came into common use, describing the lip, which in these long-lived flowers takes the distinctive form of a pouch or slipper.

This important genus has a wide distribution in the Far East, from the cool Himalayas to S. E. India, S. W. China, Burma, Borneo, Indonesia, New Guinea, the Solomon Islands and the Philippines, so the needs of various species will be met in either the warm, intermediate or cool greenhouse. As there are no pseudobulbs the compost should never be allowed to become completely dry and a light misting over the plants early in the day is beneficial in warm summer weather.

P. insigne, from the Himalayas, requires a moist, cool atmosphere in which to thrive and produce its greenish-yellow or brownish-yellow flowers with a heavy dusting of red/ brown spots on the broad dorsal (upper) sepal and also on the shiny pale-tan pouch.

Paphiopedilum insigne 'Mint Farm'

31

Pleurothallis smithiana has miniature flowers, here much enlarged

Pleurothallis species

These are sometimes referred to as 'botanical' orchids, usually by growers who like brightly coloured, impressively large flowers. However, there are many who enjoy the quiet colours and the different shapes of flowers on these often miniature plants from tropical and sub-tropical America. It is certain that Pleurothallis species will arouse interest wherever they are seen.

Rossioglossum grande

Known as the Clown Orchid because the crest on the lip has a supposed likeness to a very small clown, it has impressive large flowers, the yellow sepals barred and flecked with red-brown, the petals red-brown at the base and clear golden yellow at the ends; the flaring lip is creamy white flecked with red. Plenty of water, good humidity and moderate shade are needed when in growth but a cool, dry atmosphere when at rest.

Sophronitis coccinea

Brilliant scarlet flowers make up for the small size of this popular coolhouse species which always attracts attention whenever a well grown specimen is seen. In spring the buds appear from fat new growths before they mature and once the flowers open it is fascinating to watch them expand in size daily.

The plants are suited to pot culture or to mounting on bark or fern fibre. They must be watered with care during winter but should never be allowed to dry out completely at any time. The species has been hybridized with Laelias and Cattleyas.

Vanda coerulea

Most Vandas come from hot, humid places but this species prefers to grow either in a coolish part of the Intermediate house or a warm spot in the Cool greenhouse. The plants have narrow, leathery leaves sited neatly on each side of a stem which can grow quite tall. Aerial roots arising from the stem absorb moisture from the air and strong spikes bear several round mauvish-blue flowers 7-10cm (3-4in) across, nicely marked with darker tessellation. Plants with darkest blue flowers are the most coveted.

Zygopetalum intermedium

This is probably the finest and most widely grown species in the genus. Erect flower spikes are from immature new growths, each bearing from 3 to 7 flowers; green sepals and petals blotched with brown fan out from behind each broad white lip decorated with purple lines. This fragrant winter-flowering orchid should be given plenty of water and a modicum of fertilizer during the time when it is in active growth.

Zygopetalum hybrid

Sophronites coccinea, a small but brilliantly coloured orchid

ORCHIDS FOR THE INTERMEDIATE HOUSE

Min. night temperature 12-14°C (55-58°F)

Aerangis brachycarpa

This delightful African orchid has a fan of dark green leaves and pendent spikes bearing white, star-shaped flowers with long, pinkish spurs. More often seen is *A. confusa*, which differs only in having smaller flowers with shorter spurs.

While it is possible to grow these orchids in pots, they prosper better in baskets or mounted on bark or tree-fern.

Ansellia africana

This large African orchid has tough leaves on the upper part of tall stems. Branching spikes arching from the top of the stems bear golden

Aerangis brachycarpa
Brassavola nodosa

Ansellia africana

Brassia verrucosa

flowers with an all-over spotting of pale or dark reddish-brown, accounting for the plant's common name of 'Leopard Orchid'. Strangely, no two flowers ever seem to have the spots arranged in the same pattern.

Brassavola nodosa

The leaves are rolled like pencils on this epiphytic orchid, which often grows on cacti or mangrove roots in dry parts of Mexico, Panama and Venezuela. The very fragrant flowers have narrow, pale green sepals and petals, and a white lip spotted with red at its base. Though pot-culture is possible, the plant is best suited to mounting on cork bark where it should be watered freely when in growth, then rested after flowering. But do not let the leaves shrivel through remaining dry for too long.

Brassia verrucosa

This Central American species comes from humid forests at an altitude of up to 1600m. On plants which can grow quite massive, the long, arching spikes bear many large, spidery flowers, pale greenish-yellow in colour, spotted with dark brown.

Bulbophyllum collettii

A charming species from Burma which produces smallish pseudo-bulbs on a creeping rhizome. Short-ish spikes bear 5 or 6 flowers with pendent lower sepals between 10-13cm (4-5in) long. The petals and upper sepal are quite small, decorated with tiny tufts of fine hairs which are set into motion by the slightest breath of air. Dry winter rest is necessary, withholding water until flower spikes appear.

Cattleya loddigesii was the first cattleya to be cultivated

Cattleya species
Originating in Central and S. America, the genus is comprised of about 30 epiphytic species from a number of different climates in the wild but when in cultivation most can be grown in the Intermediate house, though a few prefer slightly cooler conditions. *C. loddigesii* was the first to be introduced into cultivation, creating a stir and firmly establishing the genus in popularity. The 8-11cm (3-4½in) pale rosy-lilac flowers have lips touched with palest yellow.

Cattleya hybrids and intergenerics
These are among the most glamorous of orchids, prized for their exotic beauty. The intermixing of genera has resulted in flowers widely varied in their colour, size and shape.

Cattleya hybrid 'La Tuilierie'

Cattleya 'Virtue' – a lovely white hybrid with golden-yellow labellum

Coelogyne pandurata

This species is known for its arching spikes of well-spaced, elegant green flowers on whose lips the ruffled crest is almost black. The flowers generally appear in autumn. The plant can be temperamental in cultivation and somewhat easier to grow is its hybrid *C. Burfordiense*, which bears larger flowers on a longer spike.

Comparettia coccinea

This small epiphyte requires humid shade; dryness about the roots should be avoided at all times. It has a slender spike bearing dainty red flowers with short curved spurs. Somewhat larger are *C. falcata*, the pink flowers of which are crisply marked with white, and *C. macroplectron* with flowers of rosy purple and white.

Cymbidium erythrostylum

As well as the 'cool' Cymbidiums already mentioned there are several from warmer parts of the Far East, and *C. erythrostylum*, from Vietnam, needs to be grown at the warm end of the Intermediate section. When it is in growth watering should be thorough with frequent addition of fertilizer. Flowering is in summer; the large flowers, pale and almost fragile looking, last for some weeks in perfection.

Dendrochilum glumaceum

An orchid with fragrant flowers is always welcome in the greenhouse and this is one of the most sweetly scented, with small white flowers crowded on spikes from among its narrow leaves. When new growths appear water should be freely given until the growth is completed.

Encyclia fragrans

This is another orchid to perfume the greenhouse. It was one of the first epiphytic orchids successfully grown and flowered in cultivation. The flowers are creamy white with fine purple stripes along the length of the lip.

Laelia harpophylla

The bright orange-red flowers of this orchid are carried above narrow leaves on thin stems; the paler lip curls back at its frilly-edged tip in a most engaging manner. The closely related *L. cinnabarina*, which grows on rocks in the wild, is similar in appearance, with cinnabar-red flowers on longer spikes. Quite different in flower colour is *L. pumila*, whose red-lipped pink flowers are on a dwarf plant scarcely more than 15cm (6in) in height. Also with pale pink flowers, *L. purpurata* is considerably larger, the plant up to 50cm (20in) tall and each flower about 15cm (6in) across. These four Brazilian orchids make a superb addition to any collection.

Lockhartia oerstedii

This is an orchid which is ornamental the year round; each long stem is completely covered by the bases of small triangular leaves along its entire length. Stems bunch close together and small, bright yellow flowers, complicated in shape, occur

Laelia harpophylla, with its brilliant orange-red flowers

from leaf axils near the top. The plants should be kept in a humid, shady spot, never becoming too dry at the roots, but requiring careful watering when not in growth.

Lycaste skinneri

This truly spectacular orchid is the national flower of Guatemala. Large deciduous leaves, up to 75cm (2½ft) long and 15cm (6in) broad are from the apex of pseudobulbs between 5-10cm (2-4in) tall. The flowers, singly on stems from the base of pseudobulbs, are very showy; soft pink sepals making a triangle behind smaller petals, much darker in colour, which incline forwards, almost hiding the lip and column. The flowers are easily bruised.

Maxillaria picta

Among long, narrow leaves, this small plant from E. Brazil carries many pale yellow flowers spotted with purplish-red. This orchid flowers in the autumn, each flower lasting for up to three weeks. One of the best known in a genus of about 300 species, it needs moderate shade and a humid atmosphere. Otherwise it is an easy-to-grow plant that increases rapidly.

Miltonia spectabilis

This well-known orchid from Brazil has the distinction of being the species on which the genus was founded. The flowers have creamy sepals and petals with a rosy flush at the base and purple lips decoratively veined with a darker shade. Grow Miltonias in pots or wooden baskets, using a compost suitable for epiphytic orchids (see pages 18-19). Restrict watering in the winter but do not allow the compost to dry out completely. They prefer semi-shade.

Maxillaria picta　　　　　*Miltonia spectabilis*

39

Miltonia 'Ambre London Conference', one of many lovely hybrids

Miltoniopsis hybrids
Whereas the Miltonias mentioned on page 39 are from Brazil, these pansy-flowered orchids have been bred from species from cooler regions in South America. The very showy flowers, in shades of red, pink, pale yellow or creamy white, have broad, prettily marked lips. Grown in shade at the coolest end of an inter-mediate house, the pale blue-green of the foliage further enhances the beauty of the flowers.

Oncidium papilio
The common name 'Butterfly Orchid' is sometimes applied to this orchid, a very apt description for the gold and orange-brown flowers with three narrow segments held high like antennae and the flowers open in succession, one at a time at the top of lengthy flexuous stems.

Oncidium papilio

Paphiopedilum acmodontum

This is one of the more recently discovered species in a genus thought to be still in the process of evolution. The large flowers, delicately tinted in modest shades of white and green flushed with purplish-pink, occur singly on stems above leaves which have their upper surfaces tessellated with light and dark green.

Paphiopedilum hybrids

The genus has been the subject of considerable interest to hybridizers and, while the flowers on many of the modern, complex hybrids are far removed from the species in colour, shape and substance, it is often possible to recognize at least some of the inherited features.

For some growers, the larger flowers, round shape and heavy substance of modern complex hybrids hold greatest appeal, while others prefer the less obvious charms of primary hybrids.

Phragmipedium caudatum

Phragmipedium caudatum

Whereas all Paphiopedilums come from the Far East the Phragmipediums, a smaller group of slipper orchids, are found only in Central and South America. The large flowers have a somewhat curious appearance, the long dorsal sepal hooded and drooping over the deep sabot-shaped lip while narrow pendent petals up to 35cm (14in) long twist gently down on each side; flower colour is pale yellowish-green and cream. The plants do best when left to make large specimens and should be kept in humid shade throughout the summer. Constant moisture around the roots can cause compost to deteriorate and it is therefore important to check for this from time to time.

Paphiopedilum 'British Bulldog'

Promenaea xanthina is a compact charmer

Promenaea xanthina

The yellow flowers of this compact orchid can brighten even the dullest day. Promenaeas look their best when encouraged to grow into specimen plants and the flowers can last up to six weeks if kept cool and heavily shaded.

Repotting should take place annually as stale conditions about the roots are actively disliked, and care must be taken not to allow water to remain on the young leaves as this can eventually lead to rotting of the plant.

Stanhopea tigrina

From 1829-1837 The Rt Hon. Philip Henry Stanhope was president of the London Medico-Botanical Society and in the year of his appointment Sir William Hooker named this genus of unusual orchids in his honour. The plants have to be grown in slatted baskets hung from glazing bars in the roof of the greenhouse so that in early summer they can push stout flower spikes down through the compost and out between the slats to reveal fat buds which will eventually become large, short-lived flowers, amazing in their complex structure and filling the air with deliciously heavy fragrance.

S. tigrina probably has the largest flowers, their base-colour of pale or dark yellow, dramatically spotted and stained with deep red.

ORCHIDS FOR THE WARM GREENHOUSE

Min. night temperature 15-18°C (60-65°F)

Aerides odoratum
This species was introduced to the Royal Botanic Gardens, Kew by Sir Joseph Banks in 1800. The fragrant pale-pink flowers set closely on arching stems are sometimes spotted and tipped with purple and have short, curved, nectar-filled spurs.

Angraecum sesquipedale
The island of Madagascar is the home of this magnificent monopodial orchid, the large white or ivory star-shaped flowers of which release a powerful sweet fragrance in the evening. This tempts the only moth with a tongue long enough to reach the nectar contained in the lower part of its lengthy spur. When well grown the plant can become rather large in a few years.

Ascocentrum ampullaceum

Ascocentrum ampullaceum
Another monopodial orchid, this small plant from Burma and Thailand has bright rose-red flowers and strap-shaped leaves which are distinctively jagged at the ends.

Angraecum sesquipedale has large, star-shaped flowers

43

Calanthe vestita stands tall, with pale, long-lasting flowers

Calanthe vestita

Tall flower stems with pale, long-lasting flowers grow from the base of pseudobulbs which have a silvery membranaceous covering and the large deciduous leaves appear after the flower spikes. This fine orchid revels in warmth and moisture about the roots.

Dendrobium phalaenopsis

This is the best known of the warmth-loving Dendrobiums, Australian in origin. Round pink flowers are on lengthy spikes from near the top of tall stems which should be grown in small pots containing very free-draining compost.

Ludisia discolor

Ludisia discolor

One of a group known as 'Jewel Orchids' because of their ornamental leaves, this has dark red leaves on which the veins gleam like liquid gold. White flowers on upright stems are a pleasing bonus. The plants should be grown in shallow pans, in full shade and watered throughout the year.

Oncidium luridum

One of the group nicknamed 'Mule Ear' Oncidiums because of the single leathery leaf on top of a small pseudobulb, this impressive species can grow to about 2m (7ft) tall, though in cultivation it seldom aspires to as much as 1m (3¼ft). The branched flower stem is extremely long and flexible and each long-lasting, dark golden flower is amazingly frilly round the edges of its sepals and petals. High light and plenty of warmth are appreciated.

Phalaenopsis hybrids

Whereas the species in this genus show their flowers in season, the hybrids seem to flower almost incessantly. Under conditions of good cultivation the dark green leaves can grow quite large and from beneath or between them strong branching flower spikes reach upwards. Buds get fat before opening to show the round flowers in shades of white, pink or yellow, some striped or speckled with contrasting colour, and the lip is always most beautiful. The spikes continue to lengthen and the plant can be in flower for several months. Warmth and humidity, with fertilizer applied fairly frequently, are the main requirements for success with these lovely orchids.

Vanda hybrids

On these monopodial orchids the round flowers can be pink, white, gold or mauvy-blue, the segments sometimes overlaid with contrasting tessellation. Given high light plus plenty of warmth and humidity they will grow and flower well and, as a bonus, usually last well.

Phalaenopsis hybrid 'Autumn Gold'

Vanda hybrid 'Thonglor'

ORCHIDS FOR THE COLD OR ALPINE HOUSE

Frost protection only

Terrestrial orchids from Europe, N. America and mountainous regions in the Far East and Japan can be successfully grown without heat if care is taken against rotting in the winter months when they are dormant. Cultivation details can be found in specialist books and journals; the following short list is merely to whet the appetite of would-be growers.

Cymbidium goeringii
From Japan, a dwarf plant with flowers singly on short stems.

Pleione hybrid 'Formasana'

Dactylorhiza **species**
Several different species, including those which can be seen flowering in many parts of Britain in late spring or early summer.

Epipactis gigantea
A vigorous species with erect stems of pinkish flowers.

Pleione **species and hybrids**
These very attractive orchids have achieved great popularity lately; due to ease of cultivation and the wide range of hybrids now available.

Dactylorhiza majalis

The Orchid Review Ltd.,
New Gate Farm,
Scotchey Lane, Stour Provost,
Gillingham, Dorset SP8 5LT

The Hon. Secretary,
British Orchid Council,
20 Newbury Drive,
Davyhulme, Manchester M31 2FA

Pleione hybrid 'Shantung'

Nurseries

McBeans Orchids Ltd.,
Cooksbridge,
Lewes, East Sussex BN8 4PR

Wyld Court Orchids,
Hampstead Norreys,
Newbury, Berkshire

Burnham Nurseries Ltd.,
Forches Cross,
Newton Abbot, Devon TQ12 6PZ

Greenaway Orchids,
Rookery Farm,
Puxton,
Nr. Weston-Super-Mare,
Avon BS24 6TL

Exmoor Orchids,
Twixtcombes,
Doverhay,
Porlock, Somerset TA24 8LL

David Stead Orchids Ltd.,
Langley Farm,
Westgate Lane,
Lofthouse,
Wakefield, West Yorkshire

Thatched Lodge Orchids,
92 Burys Bank Road,
Greenham Common North,
Newbury, Berkshire RG15 8DD

Mansell & Hatcher Ltd.,
Gragg Wood Nurseries,
Rawdon, Leeds LS19 6LQ

Stonehouse Orchid Nursery,
Ardingly,
Sussex

Woodstock Orchids,
50 Pound Hill,
Great Brickhill,
Nr. Milton Keynes,
Bucks MK17 9AS

INDEX AND ACKNOWLEDGEMENTS

Picture credits

Bruce Coleman Ltd/Eric Crichton: 39(br).
John Glover: 8, 27(br), 43(t), 45(bl).
Derek Gould: 24/5, 40(t).
Paul Harcourt Davies: 9(l,tr,br), 10(tl,tr,br), 11, 18, 26, 28, 29(b), 32.
S & O Mathews: 41(b).
Natural History Photographic Agency/Haroldo Palo: 39(bl).
Bill Pottinger; 6(t), 12(b), 14, 22, 27(t), 29(c), 33(b), 34(b), 35(tl,tr), 47.
Harry Smith Horticultural Collection: 1, 6(b), 7, 15, 19, 23(tl,tr), 27(bl), 29(t),
   31(t,b), 33(t), 36(t,b), 38, 40(b), 42, 43(b), 44(b), 45(br), 46(t,b).
Michael Warren: 4/5, 12(t), 16, 17, 30, 34(t), 37, 41(t), 43(t).

Artwork by Simon Roulstone